I SPEAK BECAUSE OF LOVE

GARY MILTON GRIFFITH SR.

Outskirts Press, Inc.
Denver, Colorado

Outskirts Press, Inc.
http://www.outskirtspress.com

ISBN: 978-1-4327-2504-4

Outskirts Press and the "OP" logo are trademarks belonging to Outskirts Press, Inc.

PRINTED IN THE UNITED STATES OF AMERICA

I speak because of love

Love has touched my mind and I can not hold back

Andrea Grayson, Editor

CONTENTS

PREFACE

Hello and welcome

It is with love I greet you all, and it is my hope that you will find some comfort and joy as you journey through these pages of love.

Many of us struggle with all types of issues in life, and at times they are misunderstood. Then a writer comes along with pen in hand and tries capturing the essences of life with its joys as well as its struggles. It's through this pen that he or she tries to convey the journey in ways to help the reader through their own experiences of life.

Inside this book I will be expressing things that I feel, delivering from my heart the things that are near and dear to me. I write poetry because it is the gift that God has given me. My source of inspiration was born from my own personal experiences in my life God has allowed, bad or good.

My prayer is that through these poems, you will be touched in your spirit and find a blessing in these words. The focus is Jesus Christ, and without Him I could not do what I do. Now find a cozy, comfortable little spot, maybe under the shade of a giant oak – or where ever it is that brings you enjoyment – and sit back and relax as you read these expressions of love. I have also included a few pictures of my family and poetically placed some recipes of the culinary arts.

You are my best love

God of love
God of mercy who is blessing me
Take me back
Renew my spirit
Take me back where I belong
I'm tired of running through life without You
You are my best love
You mean more to my life than the air I breathe
Sorry I've been disobedient
Help me to walk
Help me to stand
Lord take my hand
You are my best love
Lord before I leave this world
Before I close my eyes
I want those I come in contact with to know
That You and You alone are what defines me
It is Your standards I want to be measured by
Nothing else will do for me
Hold me in Your love
Guide me and keep me
You are my best love

Much more than words
Could ever say

How do you describe Love
What words can you use
Are they enough to show your appreciation
Is there a human thought worthy of Love
The words from your lips are they praiseworthy
I wonder do you really know
How special Love is
It is much more
Much more than words
Could ever say
As you collect your thoughts
With the words forming in your mouth
Do you really know what Love has done for us
The human experience can never do Love justice
From the hill of Golgotha
On a cross stained with the blood of Love
Love went far beyond human understanding
That's why it is much more
Much more than words
Could ever say
You could try with all your human intellect
To grasp the intimacy of love
Which you will never find
Outside of the only name worthy to be called Love
Only one
Jesus

Sometimes we forget our place in the circle of life, never stopping to think just what and who we are. It is my belief that in this vast universe that we find ourselves, we are incomplete without the loving guidance of almighty God. This is the way I feel, and you may not see it the way I do, but then again you just might. In any case, I urge you to continue reading. I also would like you to share this with others if you feel that someone you know can benefit from what you are now exploring for yourself.

Me with some of my grandchildren and my brother Robert

No one is beyond His reach

Why do you think you are not worthy?
Do you feel the wrong you have done is too great
For God in all his glory to forgive you?
When His love went beyond measure
To give us that wonderful treasure
This leads to our salvation
There have been many before you
That felt the way you do
Wondering how God could love them
No one is beyond His reach
Because His love is so deep
No one is beyond His reach
Now if you read your bible
You will find many just like you
Who all had things to go through
Disappointments and devastation
A walk through the valley of loneliness
Nevertheless, there is satisfaction
If you are willing to look and surrender
You will find the way
Not everyone will make it
Because their love and seeking is superficial
The door is still wide open
For the hearts that are willing to change
No one is beyond His reach
He is going to shake up the grave
No one is beyond His reach
It is up to you and me
To take His love into our hearts
Or miss the greatest part
His love
No one is beyond His love

We need devotion for the Lord of heaven

We need devotion for the Lord of heaven
For all He has done for us
He's far beyond the word deserving
The accolades that we give Him
Formed from the many words in our vocabulary
Even the vast number of different dialects
They can't scratch the surface of His greatness
No human words of expression can truly speak to the deity of God
We need devotion for the Lord of heaven
His many acts of kindness
The love and protection He offers us
Truly outweighs anything we can comprehend
He's given this world a treasury beyond treasuries
More precious than the air we breathe
No price tag can be placed on it
Because the love of God is beyond measure
The world doesn't know how deep God's love goes
We need devotion for the Lord of heaven
The love of God came down and dwelt among us
Many rejected and abused that Love
Love was dragged through the streets
From judgment hall to judgment hall Love was lead bound
A crown of thorns was placed on the head of Love
This caused the blood to flow
Love was stretched out on an old rugged cross
Nailed by the hands and feet
Thinking of us and not Himself
Love kept on loving through all the pain He felt
No one is more deserving of our devotion
Than the almighty

That's alright with me
God has my hand

When things don't go the way I would like
Storms of life just keep on coming
The pain of lonely love is in my heart
That's alright with me
God has my hand
He's the One who comforts me
When I'm drowning in my lonely tear drops
He's the One who helps me face the challenges
Through all of life's difficult times
Without Him I cannot make it
Even when I don't understand
That's alright with me
God has my hand
When I'm lacking in courage
Facing something I'm not ready for
Launching out into uncharted waters
No matter what it is
That's alright with me
God has my hand
He's my provider of everything I need
Giver of love, peace and joy
So whatever situation I find myself in
That's alright with me
God has my hand

I know it's alright

Jesus has it all in control
I know it's alright
Nothing will get past His hands
He watches over everything
From the small to the great
Those standing on the battlefield
As their blood is spilled
Many lives will be laid down to rest
Only to be reborn into a more glorious life
If in Jesus they sleep
I know it's alright
From our knees we give thanks
To the One who has it all in His hands
I know it's alright
You may be burdened down with a heavy load
Running short on life's necessities
Trust in Jesus Who is more precious than gold
He is your provider
I know it's alright
Whatever tomorrow is going to bring
I know it's alright
If you want to lift His name
Tell anyone that will listen
About His love and mercy
I know it's alright

My mother Joy

I believe that's what Momma would say

My children don't worry about me now
I'm doing fine in my new home
It's so beautiful here
My name says it all
There is joy in this place
If you want to see me again
Put your lives in Jesus' hands
I believe that's what momma would say
I want to see your face
All of my family in this wonderful place
There's a lot of work you all must do
Start with loving one another
Jesus will help you through
If you dare to trust and believe in Him
I believe that's what momma would say
Satan wants to rob you of your joy
Beware my family and stand on the promises of God
I believe that's what momma would say
Honor one another and love each other
Let the men in the family take their rightful place
Daughters of love guard their side
Let Jesus lead you all
Then you will see me in the Father's house
I believe that's what momma would say

8

I can only imagine

I can only imagine
What heaven will be like
I can only imagine
The face of my Master
One thing I'm sure of
My God, He is love
I can only imagine
Those streets paved with gold
I can only imagine
How He hung the stars high above
Or placed the air beneath the wings of a dove
I can only imagine
How He created everything
Look at me, look at you
We're just some of God's handy work
There's no understanding what He's done
All I know is we are here
I can only imagine
Water coming from a rock
I can only imagine
Five thousand people being fed
With two loaves of bread
I can only imagine
Jesus raising Lazarus from the dead
Turning water into wine and opening blind eyes
His power has no end, its past finding out
Awesome is my God
I can only imagine
Even my thoughts cannot do God justice
My imagination is flawed
Tainted by sin
Full of human expressions
Which cannot grasp the full scope of God's infinite design
I can only imagine

I'm not lucky
I'm blessed

My life is not left up to chance
The Master of love directs my path
Everything I have is because of Him
I'm not lucky
I'm blessed
Someone said I was in the right place at the right time
You sure must be lucky
Coincidence, no way
I'm not lucky
I'm blessed
Nothing in life happens by accident in a believer's life
There's a preconceived thought in the mind of God
Which He delivers before we even ask
That's what was meant in the word of God
When He said "I know what you need
Before you form it in your mind"
I'm not lucky
I'm blessed
I was a child about six years old
The doctor told my mother I had polio
Six long months I lay in the hospital
Look at me now
I can run, I can jump
Now I'm driving a bus
They say I'm one of the lucky ones
I'm not lucky
I'm blessed
Did you understand what I said?
Let me tell you again
I'm not lucky
I'm blessed
Nothing happens by happenstance
The sun, the moon and stars, God made them
He watches over the sparrows that fly
Rain falls from the heavens on us all
Because of His love
That's why I can say
I'm not lucky
I'm blessed

We say we are Christians

We say we are Christians
It must be more than a word
We say we are part of the Lord's body
Are our voices being heard?
Are we raising up the banner?
We should be standing on His love
Are we reaching out with compassion
With our hands covered by the blood?
We say we are Christians
Is it just on Sunday morning
That we raise our hands in praise?
We kneel at the altar of God to pray
For many so we say
God only knows
We say we are Christians
On what roads do our feet travel?
Do we walk on the same old paths?
Or do we find new ground?
Are we blazing new trails?
That others can follow
Doing things that others say are impossible?
Remember Jesus walked on the water
Peter did too
If we keep our focus
Our eyes fixed on Jesus
There will be nothing we cannot do
We say we are Christians
Then go on in the name of Jesus
Reaching all the lost souls
We are the feet
We are the arms
We are the hands of the body of Christ
We are the only Jesus many will see
So represent

The keeper of my life

I'm here in this life
It is by His design
That I'm here in His plans
My life and all that I am are in His hands
The keeper of my life
I cannot move with the rhythm of life
If He did not order my steps
The flame that burns inside my heart
Is fanned by the winds of His love
He alone holds the essence of who I am
The keeper of my life
The dreams that inhabit my mind
Songs that fill me
They come from the depths of my soul
Inspired and touched by love
Creator of all things
The keeper of my life
Some can not understand His infinite design
Nevertheless He's the only hope for mankind
It's through His blood that keeps hope alive
So I pray constantly
Thanking him earnestly
As I humble myself beneath His majesty
The keeper of my life

With life comes your chance

From the moment we are born
Life presents us with many paths to take
Some are beyond our control
As we lay in our infinite state
Dependent on those around us
To guide and to nurture
Until we can stand on our own
Then we must choose and choose wisely
Because there are many forks in the road
With life comes your chance
A chance to live a life that's free
A chance to touch a heart
To win or to lose
With life comes your chance
The question that plagues us all
Is how will we respond to life?
Will we merely take it for granted
Or accomplish something that's really worthwhile?
Remember **with life comes your chance**
To make a difference in the lives of many
An example for others to follow
Good or bad
The decision is yours
To be a positive influence or a negative one
True leaders inspire
This lifts the hopes and dreams of others higher
This will in turn create new leaders
Men and women who are more than just dreamers
So don't waste your time
With life comes your chance

Gary's Smokin' Greens

Ingredients:
- 3-4 Smoked turkey wings
- 1 large Yellow onion
- 1 tsp Crushed chili peppers or 1-2 chopped Fresno chilies
- 1 tbsp Garlic granulated or fresh chopped
- Lawry's seasoned salt (start with 1 tsp)
- Greens – 4 bunches each of Mustard, Collard, Swiss chard & Spanish, Triple washed, then to have the proper mix put greens into large plastic bag and mix well. Tip: you can buy triple washed greens in plastic bags.

Now you are ready to begin.
Place turkey in a large pot with enough water to cover by about 1 inch. Add all ingredients except the greens, place on stove on med heat and cook for 30 minutes covered. Add greens to about 1 inch from top of pot. Replace cover. Keep an eye out so that your pot does not boil over. Let greens cook down then add more. Repeat until all greens have been added. Let simmer for 1 to 2 hours, stirring every 20 minutes and tasting to make sure the taste is to your liking.

Optional:
You may use smoked neck bones or ham hocks instead of turkey. Also, you can add bacon ends to add more meat and flavor, but if you choose to do so remember bacon has salt, so take care not to add too much salt.

Note: If ham hocks are used, cook 1 hour on med heat, add onion and all the other spices, then a half hour later start adding your greens.

Enjoy!

14

You alone have set me free

When I was down and didn't understand
You lifted me from the trouble I was in
Gave Your life on Calvary
You alone have set me free
Mother prayed that one day I would see
That holding His hand is life's guaranty
Many dark days and trials I would face
Look at me now as I run this race
Things I go through are nothing but a test
Common to the whole human race
To build me up and make me strong
So I can live on
To share my testimony about You, Lord of Glory
How that through Your death You rescued me
You alone have set me free
Now many will suffer hardship envy and strife
Some will rise and others will fall
Only through Jesus can you survive
The journey may be long and hard
Tears will fill your eyes
Don't give up
Stand and fight
You will be victorious
Just like me
Then you will say
I know it's You, Jesus
No one else will do
You alone have set me free

Late night conversation

In the middle of the night
When I'm all alone
That's my time
To lay it all on the line
In my room of solitude
I bare my soul
To the One Who hears my plea
He never compares me to another
Allowing me to be me
He's my greatest lover
You don't know the **late night conversation**
That I have with the King of creation
From Him I could never hide who I am
I am naked in His sight
Totally exposed before His mighty hand
That's why I can share all my sorrows
Giving Him the deepest part of me
Which you may never see
Because you're wrapped up just like me
Born of a woman shaped in iniquity
You don't know the **late night conversation**
I share with the Lord of my salvation
On my knees with deep supplication
In complete submission to the One Who holds my tomorrow
I pray earnestly to Him
You don't know the **late night conversation**
That I have with the Lord of the resurrection
Who promised me a crown
If I keep Him first in my life
To His will I must stay in complete subjection
From my bended knees I can see Him better
Humbling myself beneath His power
In the middle of the night I have my **late night conversation**

Hello first born

Hello first born
Have I told you lately that I love you
You mean so much to me
It was God that blessed me with your smile
I wonder if you can truly see
Even if I was on a desert isle
My love for you is deeply embedded
Nothing on earth can take that away
Heaven has a place for us
Hello first born
I'm so glad to be your dad
It's a wonderful journey
One day we will dance among the stars
With Jesus, our number one
Put all your hopes in Him
Not me, because I will fail you
He will keep your light from growing dim
Even if I fail my love will always be
Because I love you my dear daughter
Hello first born
I'm here with all my imperfection
When you need me call
I'll say it again
Love is fully saturated in me
It's distributed equally
Among all my children
But this one's for you
I love you
Hello first born

Daddy cares

I know it seems hard to understand
That life can be so painful
Baby girl you just have to stand
You are stronger than you think
Don't think for a moment that you stand alone
I'm here with you, and I'm on my knees
Even though there are many miles between us
Through the eyes of Jesus I can see
Daddy cares
I love you with all my heart
My dream is to one day have you here
I need you to step up and grab life by the horns
There's so much strength in you
It's been there since you were born
I know life can be so ruff
But I know you are tuff enough
Daddy cares
There is nothing you cannot do
But you must believe in yourself
Then the God of heaven will see you through
I can't give you everything on a platter
Things just don't work that way
I give my love the only thing that matters
So baby girl I want you to know
Daddy cares

Don't settle for nothing less

In this ever changing world
You can find your place in the Son
Never short change yourself
Where are you going to run?
There is so much awaiting you
Just immerse yourself in the waters of love
Don't settle for nothing less
In the hands of God you can find who you are
More than what the devil has in store
Jesus died so you can be free
Step up now and guide your family
Baby boy, you can make it if you try
His hands are open, can't you see?
Don't settle for nothing less
Many nights and so many tears
On my knees I pray for you constantly
My God I know he hears
From His throne He smiles down on me
He's God and He does not lie
So son open your eyes
This world will soon pass you by
Grab all that God has to give
Don't settle for nothing less
You have my love
Most of all Jesus loves you
The evidence is on that blood-stained cross
Stand and be a leader to your children
God paid the cost
So your family and you won't be lost
Don't settle for nothing less

Are You pleased with me today?

Lord are You pleased with me today?
Stand by me
Help me to walk in Your way
Keep me humble and depending on You
My life, I know it's not perfect
I make no claims to that
Just want to be pleasing in Your sight
Are You pleased with me today?
From the corners of my mind
Am I constantly thinking of You?
Do You inhabit my dreams and every part of me?
From my lips do I represent You?
Is my heart totally Yours
Or do my thoughts betray me?
Is my outward appearance only a façade?
You, Lord, I can never deceive
Because You pierce my soul with Your all-seeing eyes
Going deep where no man can see
Are You pleased with me today?
I must be careful in the way I honor You
To be pleasing it's not about me
It's the way I care for others
I must deny myself so You can shine
To be like You, Jesus
I must push my pride to the rear
Allow You to reign over every part of me
It's not about tomorrow for me
That day may never come
It's what I do today for You Lord that really matters
Are You pleased with me today?

How do you say that

How do you say that you love God
Don't you know words are not enough
How do you say that He's on your side
When you sit and watch someone go through times that are tuff
Are you sure God is with you
How do you say that
Do you know it's not the words you use
It must be a heart-felt condition
That only God and you know the truth of it all
How do you say that you love the Lord
When you can't love your neighbor
Sitting on the pews showing your indifference
I know it's what you have learned
From someone, maybe even a preacher
Come on, you must show some temperance
Trust in God, not in man
Man will lie to you and abuse you
Guard your heart with the tenderness of the Lord
Guard your mind from this world's subtle distractions
Then you can walk and talk as you represent Christ
By truly living the life
How do you say that you live in Christ and Christ in you
I'm sure your actions are speaking loudly
One way or the other
Do you click with those who share a similar pigmentation
Do you render judgments for the sins of the past
Never considering your own
Do you look down on those who look like they have less
Are you willing to share of your possessions
Yet you say you love the Lord

How do you say that
When from your lips comes deceit and condemnation
Showing no affection for the lost or those suffering degradation
You just pile on them your self-righteousness
Why should they feel humiliation
From someone who says they love the Lord
How do you say that you're a child of the King
"I'm a born again Christian"
When your life does not point the way
Who are you serving, God or yourself
Maybe something else
As you think about it
Ask yourself the question
"How do I say that I'm in God's hands"
Be careful of your answer
Pray for God's strength in your life
Pray for His love and protection to rule your heart
Then when someone ask you
How do you say that
Confidently you can say "in and through the Lord Jesus"

How can you stand by and do nothing

What's wrong with your heart
Do you harbor compassion in there
When you see a soul reaching out
Holding a sign "will work for food"
Is that dollar, **if you give it**, going to break you
Are you worried that they will do wrong with it
That little dollar you give
Then pray to the God of heaven
To touch their hearts and minds
You just need to let your compassion flow
How can you stand by and do nothing
When you see a child torn from a mothers arms
You know kidnapping it's a crime
How can you turn and look away
What if they were one of yours
Tell me how you would feel then
How can you stand by and do nothing
Some watch from their windows
Children playing in the neighborhood
While drugs are being sold by the local hood
You pull closed the curtains as you close your eyes
Hoping the problem will go away
How can you stand by and do nothing
Suddenly violence erupts
Because of the lost and corrupted
A stray bullet touches one of yours
Then you get involved
Only too late, another is gone
You line the streets in front of city hall
Holding signs that read
"Stop the violence"
"Save our children"
When you could have done something sooner
God gives us choices
How can you stand by and do nothing

It's examination time

It's examination time

Time to turn the spotlight on ourselves, because when we are in the light we can't hide, it will illuminate all the cracks and blemishes on our faces, that's why actors and actresses wear make-up to try and hide unsightly scars, because when the heat is on make-up melts away leaving the real you.

We need to be sure God is pleased with us, when we leave this world behind it will be too late to renew our minds, so while it is day and the blood is pumping through our veins, we need to do all we can in the service of the Lord.

<u>Point #1 – In order to examine ourselves we must first know and believe that we need God; we must also be humble enough to admit our weaknesses and our faults.</u>

Gal. 6:4
It's examination time

The word of God tells us to examine our hearts, we need to look into the mirror and really see who we are, and do we truly believe in what we say we believe when it comes to the things of God. Point #2 – We should never compare ourselves or our weaknesses to others, because God has work for each of us, and our trials and weaknesses are tailored, and God grades us on our own merits and not those of others.

1 Cor. 11:28
It's examination time

We need to do like David did, we need to seek like David did, he knew he was a wretch, undone, so he would shout out to the Lord, "create in me a clean heart", oh yes he did.

Point #3 – When we come to the altar of God, or when we partake in the Lord's supper, we must test our condition in Christ, our spiritual condition, because when we hold grudges, unforgiveness in our hearts, we will lack commitment to God and our repentance will not be full. My brothers and sisters, are you hearing me?

1 Cor. 9:27
It's examination time

We need to make sure we're not dead men walking, because that condition only leads to a life of misery, in this life and in the life to come.

Point #4 – Examining ourselves will help us to discipline our body, mind and spirit so we can do the work God would have us to do. Without discipline we will never be what God wants us to be.

Ezekiel 37 and Matt. 23:27
It's examination time

We're coming to the closing now but not the end.
In Ezekiel he talks about the valley of dry bones, we don't want to be like those bones, dead and lifeless, serving no purpose. What good would it be to live your life only looking good on the outside, when on the inside you're nothing but dead men's bones, not knowing who you are, can't praise God and rejoice with someone else when they are praising God? If this is you then you need to check yourself. You see when the Spirit is moving, it will move the bones that are sitting in the pews or standing next to you. If they don't move then what God are they serving, because the word of God tells me that the Spirit will quicken dead bones.

Point #5 – This is the last point I want to make. God can revitalize old, dried up, dead and stinking bones, but He's not going to force anyone to serve Him. You need to choose for yourself who you will serve: either serve God or do your own thing.

Big G's Fajitas

Poetry never tasted so good!
Here's a recipe by me your author, for chicken or beef fajitas,
enough for a party.

Ingredients:
- 5 lbs boneless chicken breast or beef flank steaks
- Chili powder
- Lawry's seasoned salt
- Ground Cumin
- Cayenne pepper
- Yellow onions, sliced
- Bell peppers, 3 colors, sliced
- Mushrooms, sliced
- Cilantro, chopped
- Lemon juice in squeeze bottle to use on each layer
- Concentrated orange juice defrosted to pour over each layer
- Beer 6 to12 oz per layer (enough to slightly cover each layer)
- Flour fajita sized tortillas

Preparation and cooking instructions:
Trim any excess fat and wash meat. In a large container layer all the ingredients in order listed (except tortillas), then let marinate over night. Bake or grill the meat (if baked, oven temperature should be about 350 to 375 degrees) until done (cooking times will vary depending on meat thickness, etc., so check every 15 to 20 minutes). After meats are done set aside. Slice up fresh bell peppers, mushrooms and onions and sauté. You may add other vegetables if you like but don't over do it, it's all about the poetry of cooking, have fun. Slice your meats in the desired thickness that you want after all it's your party (but not too thick, and not too thin). Serve hot and enjoy!

What do you think is going to happen
When the sky unrolls

People I'm writing these words to ask you a question
Can you imagine what you will be doing
On that day of the Lord
The day of the Lord is when Jesus returns
What do you think is going to happen
When the sky unrolls
Do you believe that there will be a day like that
Have you ever heard of Russian Roulette
Are you sure you really want to take that chance
Go on ahead and spin that chamber
Then after your rude awakening
I don't want you to be full of anger
Because you had your chance to grab that anchor
But you chose not to believe in His return
What do you think you will be doing
Do you think you will be running around
Spending money all around the town
Maybe you will be watching them score touchdowns
Men you feel are part of the elite
But all will fall unless we confess and bow at His feet
It's just a warning I'm trying to convey
In the hope that everyone will not go astray
What do you think is going to happen
When the sky unrolls
I believe it will be the biggest event the world has ever known
Beyond any story ever told
Are you secured or unsecured
It's up to you

You need to learn to lean
Lean on Him

I know it seems hard to totally trust
In that name of Jesus
You wonder what is all the fuss
Is He nothing but a myth
In Him believe you must
Your lives depend on what you do
You need to learn to lean
Lean on Him
Sometimes standing on God's principles
Seems so hard
Almost impossible
You're not the first to go down that road
You won't be the last
Having faith in something you can't see
Defies human understanding
Now if you dare to move beyond the confines of your mind
To embrace the love of Jesus
You will find more than you can contain
So much praise
Which the birds and all of nature sing
They don't worry about tomorrow
Trusting and depending on Him
Is what they do
Why not you
You need to learn to lean
Lean on Him

Healer of all wounds

Lonely hearts as you walk out into the rain
You may be trying to hide your tears
God understands your pain
It doesn't matter what you're going through
Hole in your heart
It feels like it's never been filled
You feel so very empty
He's there standing with open arms
Healer of all wounds
You're sitting at the dinner table
Giving thanks to the Lord right before your meal
When the telephone rings
It's your brother with some heart wrenching news
Momma is gone
You can't believe it
Deep inside you just refuse
Then you hang up the phone as the tears begin to flow
You run to your room
Fall to your knees on the side of the bed
Why, why, why, as you hold the bible and her picture in your hands
"She's only sleeping, not dead"
Comforting words you receive from the Lord
Healer of all wounds
Your child is born and joy fills your heart
Through the years you watch him grow
Wondering what he might grow to be
Love for him everyday you show
Then one day your lives are shattered
Sitting in the court room the judge says ten years
You fall out, laying there on the floor
With tears in your eyes you look towards heaven
Then you hear the voice of the Lord
Saying "I have you and him in my hands
There is no need to worry
Let me do what I do best
I'm your friend and comforter
I Am"
Healer of all wounds

32

I'm sure of His love

In this fast moving world
There are so many choices
It really has my head in a whirl
I don't know about you
There is one thing that I'm sure of
I'm sure of His love
He picks me up when I'm down
Keeps me when I can't keep myself
When I felt like I was at a breakdown
I looked back to the cross
It was there He took all the pain to Himself
In my life He is my Logos
There is so much beauty and wisdom
In just the utterance of His name
When a child is born
With the air filling its lungs for the first time
The mother holding the child gently to her chest
It just makes me know how wonderful He is
I'm sure of His love
When I need the strength of love to be my fortress
I can count on Him to go the distance
Protect me from the reckless
Without Him my life has no balance
Then there is no meaning
So glad that is not the case
I'm sure of His love

The chosen ones

We have a great opportunity that lies before us
A chance to shake up the world
To make a difference in the lives of so many
Showing the world that love is alive
Because we are an example of that love
We are **the chosen ones**
On a mission for God
Not because we are better than anyone
It's because we like so many others heard the call
Then we responded as we fell to our knees
So many people are counting on us
It's the way we show our selves as we cross their paths
We may never see them again
The impression that we leave on them
Will be something that will last a lifetime
We are **the chosen ones**
Representatives of the King of kings
The One who paid with divine blood
Setting in motion for all times
For all people no matter what creed or color
That wonderful gift of salvation
The chance to live again
Many have lost hope of a decent life
War torn countries with the stench of death
People standing in doorways trying to escape falling debris
All around the world the cry is the same
Park benches are where you will find masses yearning to be free
There is a lot of work to be done
A lot of hearts to touch, mouths to feed and friends to gain
Are we ready to roll up our sleeves?
To get down and dirty
Are we one?
The ones they call **the chosen ones**

I don't have to cry no more

One day my journey will be over
I will dance on those streets of gold
Mother will be there to hold
But most of all I will see my Lord
He will take all the pain away
That's why I can say
I don't have to cry no more
He will meet me at the door
I'm talking about those pearly gates
That stand before His heavenly throne
On that day that I go home
I don't have to cry no more
No more disappointments
Joy will be over flowing
Love and praise will be on the lips of everyone
No more belonging to a denomination
You will not be judged by the color of your skin
Or the clothing that you're in
Fake will not be the way
We will be greeted with love
Treated with respect
What a place that will be
I don't have to cry no more

The writer

In life there are many paths that people take
Some walk the high road
Others travel low to the ground
They all have stories that must be told
Inventors and singers who carry a tune
Doctors, dancers and those who make us laugh
Where would we all be without **the writer** and his pen
The writer puts the words to the melody of a song
From Broadway to Hollywood
The writer's works are known
Acting out on stages and singing their songs
What kind of world would we live in if **the writer** was gone
No newspapers or magazines
How could they cram for an exam if **the writer** wasn't here
But we are here to share for your enjoyment
You can open a book and laugh and cheer
As you relax in your favorite chair
Lose yourselves for hours in the pages that you read
As you identify with **the writer** and his dream
Not everyone can sing and dance
We all are not doctors or what ever the trade
But I'm one of them who loves to make you smile
Or bring tears to your eyes
I'm **the writer**

Why do you look for a superhero

Down through the annals of time
Man has always tried to find
Something better than himself
Not willing to accept the Divine
Creating for himself super fantasies
Extraordinary men
With beyond belief abilities
Why do you look for a superhero
Is it because there is something that you fear
Have you truly looked deep within
Probing what it is that motivates your every notion
I know sometimes life can get under your skin
So you fantasize about people and things
In the hope of escaping the commotion
Why do you look for a superhero
You search so very hard among the human race
Looking for that ultimate "S"
On somebody's chest
Which you will not find
Because you fail to recognize
That there has already been One
Oh yes, and only One
A star from heaven
With powers beyond our wildest dreams
One of us, but above us
The Creator of the world
Who has provided us true freedom beyond the grave
Not forcing it but giving it to us as a gift
Why do you look for a superhero
When One has already been given
The Son Who is risen

What can we do without Him

I don't know how you do it
Waking up every morning
Living your life like you just don't have a care
How far do you think you will get
Can you make it from beyond the grave
Don't sit or walk around in a daze
What can you do without Him
You can think that you're doing it on your own
Like turning the wheel as you drive your car
Are you really in control
Anything and everything
From the simplest of tasks
To the most complex
He is the Master Organizer of life
It is foolish to think otherwise
What can we do without Him
There is really nothing we can do
We need Him for the air we breathe
And for the food that sustains our existence
Most of all we need Him for the salvation of our souls
To secure our heavenly home
What can we do without Him
Nothing

Drowning is not an option

As long as I live
No matter how I'm feeling
I can't go under
Drowning is not an option
The water may rise higher and higher
Feels like I'm going down for the last time
Waiting seems so hard to do
My patience is running thin
But in life we all must face adversity
Stand when we feel empty
When our hearts are broken
It is here where the Designer of life will meet us
Things that are broken can be fixed
Drowning is not an option
Now when the flood waters are raging
Debris all around us
Caught in the swiftness of its current
A decision must be made
In the face of sure disaster
Only one way out
Calling on the name of Jesus
Will turn the situation about
His hands will lift me from troubled waters
As long as there is hope
Drowning is not an option

Why do you talk about me

You see me on the street corners
Sometimes I'm in my satin red
High heel pumps but my lays are sturdy
Once in awhile I see the jailers
I don't know how I got caught up but there are mouths to be fed
Why do you talk about me
This is all that I know
I cry everyday for a solution
In my world there are not that many choices
Like those before me I'm trapped in this condition
Why do you talk about me
I'm walking down the street in my baggy clothes
Earphones in my ears and my head bobbing up and down
Just because I don't look like you
You give me that look and pass me by
Turn to your friends and begin to talk
You don't know who I am
Why do you talk about me
I sit behind walls of steel
Let me tell you what I feel
It's like being locked in a room
They have thrown away the key and there's no way out
No happy sounds or smiling faces
It would be nice to get a letter or two
Is it that you just don't care
I'm your father, mother, brother, sister, friend
All I do is thank God everyday
That He is on the throne
Why do you talk about me

Facing who I am keeps me depending on Jesus

There are so many paths in life that we can take
Where the roads are not always smooth
Some lead to nowhere
Many are meant to confuse and cast illusion
The corridor of life has so many avenues
Yet we have choices
We are free will agents with a dilemma
There are many voices clamoring for our attention
Makes you feel like throwing your hands in the air
Saying you just don't care
You know knowledge is power
We perish for lack of it
True knowledge is from the Divine
Who makes no mistakes
I've come to understand my place in the grand scheme of things
It's not about me or any of my counter parts
Facing who I am keeps me depending on Jesus
After all, everything was created for and by Him
When we read the life signs
Everything points to the Lord Jesus
Without Him I cease to exist
How can I live in this world He created
With a self-centered attitude
Trying to get mine
The phrase today is getting paid
When the price has already been laid
Facing who I am keeps me depending on Jesus
In the midst of all the pain that comes my way
All the calamity and joy
I find peace in surrendering to the Lord Jesus
Who is my strength

My joy was never lost

I wonder have you ever felt discouraged
Seems like time itself was against you
The joy of youth being siphoned from your body
Well I felt that way before
But I had it twisted
Life is not always a bed of roses
The Master Himself had days of despair
Crying in the garden
So our joy may be full
My joy was never lost
What I thought was disappointment
Was only life's proving ground
Preparing me for my ultimate journey
To the place where love and joy reigns supreme
So until then I will live life with expectancy
Crying and laughing sometimes
Taking the pains of life in stride
They say no one lives forever
I don't believe that
I know there's life after I close my eyes
There are only two places our souls will go
Don't be deceived brothers and sisters
We will end up in one of them
For that choice I'm truly thankful
Because of who He is
My joy was never lost

Beneath the sounds I can not hear

One day we will arrive at a place
Somewhere we all will pass by
Under the sounds of crickets in the night
A place where people bow to the heavens
Where birds sing by day
A place where sunshine and rain will fall
Under the shade of a giant oak
Or beside the serenity of a gentle brook
In a place pleasing to the eyes
Where the sounds of the day go unnoticed
By all who rest here
Waiting to hear once again
To hear that voice of the Master
When I like many will rise from our sleep
To bask in the warmth of the Son
Until then I will rest
Beneath the sounds I can not hear

Smoking R G Pot Roast

Ingredients:
- One 4 pound boneless beef chuck roast or bottom round rump
- ¼ teaspoon seasoned salt, more for taste if desired
- ¼ teaspoon black pepper
- ¼ teaspoon cayenne pepper
- ½ cup all purpose flour
- ½ cup canola oil
- 3 med onions, one chopped the others cut in quarters
- 3 garlic cloves, chopped
- 1 medium green bell pepper, chopped
- 2 medium jalapeno peppers, chopped
- 4 celery ribs cut into 2 inch lengths
- 14 baby carrots
- 9 small red potatoes, scrubbed but unpeeled
- 2 cups of beef broth
- 2 cups of filtered or bottled water
- 6 oz of beer
- 1 large Dutch oven which will be used to sauté and bake in the oven

Cooking instructions:
Preheat oven to 325 degrees. Season your roast with seasoned salt, cayenne pepper and black pepper. Roll roast in flour, shake off excess and save for your gravy later. Add 2 tablespoons of oil to the Dutch oven and brown your roast on all sides, about 10 minutes or so. Remove roast, set aside, then add remaining oil and sauté all of your chopped vegetables about 5 minutes. Return roast to pot, add beef broth, beer and one cup of water. Place in oven covered and bake 2 hours, turning meat every 15 to 20 minutes. After 2 hours add your quartered onions, celery, baby carrots and red potatoes and bake for another 30 to 45 minutes. Take from oven, remove the roast and vegetables and place them in another container and cover. Skim off the fat from the liquid. Take the flour that was left and on the stove make your gravy using the pot liquor (the remaining liquid). Start with a ½ cup of liquid or use it all, season to taste. Carve roast. Return carved roast and vegetables to pot once gravy is ready and simmer 5 to 10 minutes. Serve hot!

Darker than blue

We are in a box that others have made for us
The sad thing
Is that we contributed to its design
After those that have given so much to change the shape of the box
We still struggle within
Yes we are a people **darker than blue**
There is still much work to do
We must change the way others view us
By rebalancing the negative things that surround us
Learn to control our unbridled passion
So we don't fall prey and give in to weakness
Darker than blue
You can say that
We as a people must make choices that will elevate
Do things that will change our direction
We must teach love and set the example
Show our young there is a better way
Nothing is settled with the taking of life
Darker than blue
That's what we are
We can't let what they think about us be true
Some see us as gang bangers
Or either drug dealers, prostitutes and pimps
If we play a sport
We become someone's meal ticket
So what if we can't read or write well
It hurts nothing but our integrity
We are much more than that
If we only believe
We can soar to greater heights
It is a wonderful thing to be gifted and Black
Let's remember to gain knowledge
Help our children to go to college
Let the dignity of who we are flourish
In the hand and under the watchful eye of God

Black heritage

Black heritage is something to be proud of
Not to the point of thinking you are better than anyone
But that you can contribute to the world you love
For through the struggles of life was born determination
When the forces of evil were trying to stop your progress
Truth and freedom marched on in spite of complications
So that the hopes and dreams of our future would not digress
Black heritage is just one part of the greater whole
With every part being equal
Black heritage is thanking God for who we are
Because we all have something to do to help the next man
Those on the scene long after we are gone
Leaving a legacy that they can improve on
There is one thing that is clear
To be proud of your heritage is to keep God first
Because without Him there is no us
So when you stand up remember who you are
We are created in His image
To Him we all will bow one way or the other
So don't get caught up in all the hoop-la
Black heritage is a good thing
Let's keep it in its proper place
So we as a people can truly rise
To live out our full potential
Stay up and stay blessed
Then we can truly enjoy our **Black heritage**

Black determination

My people
Don't give up on your dreams
Instead check what drives your engine
What is it that motivates you
Are you here to inspire
Or are you just a spectator
Never really getting into the game
Allowing what they did before you to pass you by
Many years of blood spilt from the bodies of your past
It would be a shame to let that **Black determination** vanish
Don't you think we have a lot to be thankful for
We should be on our knees everyday
Thanking God for directing the steps of those whose sweat saturated the ground
So much **Black determination**
This inspired the hearts of many
They could not fight back the tears
Exchanging salty kisses
They embraced one another
Yearning to see their people free
They climbed aboard that freedom train
Black determination forging ever forward
Like a mother giving birth to her child
Knowing that she must endure the pain
With the birth the pain does not end
Now she watches over her young child
Standing through the night
Like a soldier on guard without a smile
Black determination
Pushing until we all can stand side by side
In love and harmony and never stopping
Black determination

I'm moving on and there's nothing you can do

I'm moving on and there's nothing you can do
Thirty million strong are pushing me
I hear the voices of those who were before
Courageous Black men and women
Hoping that we would heed the call
Add to this world
Something that every race would enjoy
Driven by love
In the hope of peace
What are we going to do?
Keep bringing each other down
Or bring something that would inspire?
I'm moving on and there's nothing you can do
My life is not mine by myself
It belongs to God
No matter if I'm wrong or right
He has the final say
I don't want to waste my time
Leading somebody to the Lord is the ultimate
Giving them a chance to live again
It's beyond me
What I do in His service
It's not up to you to judge
Will you be found in His Bosom?
Will you make a difference?
It's time to stand up
I'm moving on and there's nothing you can do

Glo's Chicken Adobo

Ingredients:
- 8 assorted pieces of frying chicken
- 1 med yellow onion, chopped
- 6 cloves of garlic, chopped
- 1 qt chicken or beef broth
- ¼ cup soy sauce
- ¼ cup lemon juice
- ¼ cup sugar
- 1 pt brandy (optional)
- 4 bay leaves

Cooking instructions:
Combine all ingredients in a large pot. Bring to a boil, and then reduce heat. Cover and cook slowly until chicken is tender.

Remove bay leaves. Serve in bowls over rice. – Enjoy

Options: to spice it up, try adding crushed chili peppers or jalapeno peppers. Also try adding chopped celery and/or mushrooms.

Since all the alcohol burns off, dish is very tasty with brandy!

Poetic Seafood Delight

Ingredients:
A delightful blend of mussels, shrimp, crab, scallops, octopus and calamari, ¼ pound of each
1 yellow onion, chopped
2 jalapeno peppers, chopped
2 cups of chopped mushrooms
2 stalks of celery, chopped
½ teaspoon of olive oil
1 16oz can of stewed tomatoes
1 16oz can tomato sauce
1 teaspoon of granulated garlic
½ teaspoon seasoned salt
2 cloves fresh chopped garlic (optional)

Cooking instructions:
Combine oil, seafood and chopped vegetables in a large skillet and sauté about 4-5 minutes on med heat. Stir in remaining ingredients and simmer about 30-60 minutes, stirring often.

Serve over pasta or rice.

Options:
Try using cream of mushroom or cream of celery soup in place of stewed tomatoes and tomato sauce, about 2 cans (or make your own from scratch), be creative and have fun.

To all my family and friends
From your poet

Potato Casserole

This is a rib sticking meal. It will fill you up, and it's quick and easy. Enjoy for dinner on a cold winter night as you cuddle by the fire.

Ingredients:
- 6 large potatoes
- 1 ½ pounds lean ground beef
- Seasoning salt
- Garlic powder
- 1 whole onion
- Black pepper
- Onion powder
- Cayenne pepper
- 1 can of cream of mushroom soup
- 1 can of filtered or bottled water

Slice potatoes ¼ inch thick. Once all potatoes are sliced...season to taste
Chop onion and add to ground beef, add seasoning to ground beef and mix with hands. Then create patties to what ever size you like
In a 10 inch pan add a layer of potatoes followed by a layer of ground beef patties. Continue to layer potatoes and ground beef patties until meat and potatoes are gone.
Take cream of mushroom soup and mix in a bowl with water then pour over casserole.
Bake at 350 for 40 minutes or until potatoes are soft.

Let's all stay together

Hey family
One day the heartaches will be over
Let's all stay together
Like Grandma wanted us to
We can make it
We have a lot to hold on to
It will get us through the rainy days
When those storm clouds come
Pain is a fact of life and we will endure
We are never alone
The Master is always watching over us
Together we can stand
Like pillars beneath a building
We can hold each other up
Let's all stay together
Can't you hear their voices
Crying out so earnestly
"Love one another and hold on to God
Because that day is going to come
When all the faithful children of God will come together
We want to see you there
To dance with you
Sing and laugh as we jump for joy
Beneath the might throne of God"
Let's all stay together
Make it your plan and desire
To attend the greatest reunion
Sitting around that campfire
Will you be there
Let's all stay together

Dedicated to the family and friends of Erma Miller

I have love overflowing in my heart

Love is so precious
Jesus gave it to me
So I can share it with you
In the hope that you will hear and understand
The words that come from my heart
It's not about me
I'm only a vessel proclaiming the Lord Jesus Christ
Who gave His undying love
Because of love
Now I can boldly say
I have love overflowing in my heart
Oh what floods of joy I feel
To know that God in his infinite wisdom
Would use someone like me
To tell the world about His love
I'm nobody special
With flaws just like you
I have accepted His gift of love
This has set me free
Forgave me of everything because I asked
Now there's no hesitation when I say
I have love overflowing in my heart
He moves me in a wonderful way
I pray that one day
God's love will resonate from your lips
When your heart has become full of His love
The joy that's indescribable has gripped your soul
Then you will shout to the world
About a King, a God, a Savior so real
Then you will say just like me
I have love overflowing in my heart

I can't make it without You

What am I without You
How can I hope to make it
Outside of You I'm nothing
You complete every part of me
I can't make it without You
My life is totally depended on You
I need You to walk with me
To lead me through this land
Pick me up when I fall
As often as I do
I can't make it without You
Without the air I breathe there's no life in me
I'm like the grass nourished by the morning dew
Like flowers bathing in the rain
They seem to dance at the rising of the sun
As they sway in the gentle breeze
It feels good to be warmed by the sun
Nature and all its wonders needs You
Just like I do
I can't make it without You
From the mountains that stand guard over the valleys
To the stars that adorn the heavens
They all sing praises to Who You are
And like them
I can't make it without You

I can win
When I stand

I don't have to be a victim
I have the right to choose
What I allow in my life
Knowing that You have the final say
Do I flourish in the day
Or hide under the cover of night
I can win
When I stand
Allow Your principles to truly motivate
Keep me on that path
Where I can find peace and joy
I can never be perfect
You're not asking that of me
I just need to acknowledge
That there is something greater than myself
On both ends of the spectrum
One trying to destroy me
The other looking out for my good
I can win
When I stand
I need to stay connected
Bend my knees everyday
Close my eyes and see You
Lose myself in Your reflection
See myself through Your eyes
Then thank You
I can win
When I stand

Paprika Chicken

Ingredients:
- 2 pounds chicken wings or boneless thighs
- Paprika
- Salt
- Black pepper
- Garlic powder
- Cayenne pepper
- 1 onion
- 1 bell pepper
- 1 container of sour cream
- 1 tablespoon canola oil
- 2 tablespoons all purpose flour

Cooking instructions:
Chop onion and bell pepper, add oil and sauté in pot about 5 minutes on medium heat. Season chicken with salt, pepper, garlic powder and cayenne pepper. Add chicken to pot with the sautéed veggies and stir. Add paprika, make sure all the chicken is coated well with the paprika. Cook on medium heat for about 30 minutes or until chicken is completely done. Add all purpose flour to container of sour cream and mix well. Stir the sour cream into the pot with the chicken, now it is ready.
Try serving it over white rice or over pasta.

Options: You can also use your favorite cream soups instead of the sour cream.

Holding my head in my hands

Holding my head in my hands
Tears running down my face
Crying my eyes out
For the wrong I have done
Pain gripping my heart
Sad eyes all around me
Seems like I've let them down
Nothing pains me more
Than the vow that lies broken
So down on my knees I pray
Holding my head in my hands
Forgive me, my sweet Lord
Don't hide Your face from me
I know it's Your grace and mercy
I feel like I don't deserve it
So glad it's You on the throne
Hallelujah
Sometimes I fall
It's You that helps me stand
Holding my head in my hands
Eyes all puffy and red
You understand my tears
Keep on holding me up with Your love
I know I'm covered by Your blood
It gets hard sometimes
It feels like I just can't make it
You transcend my darkest hours
There You are holding my hand
Comforting me like no one can
Holding my head in my hands
The tears may flow at times
In Your arms I know I'm safe
You never fail
Thank You Jesus

Hidden beneath Your shadow

Hidden beneath Your shadow
That's where I want to be
It's not me that's important
Lord it's all about You
As I melt away
Let me hide myself in Thee
Let everything in me point the way to You
Without You my life is empty
Only You can fill that void
So with You I'm going to stay
Hidden beneath Your shadow
So glad You cover me
You bear all my burdens
You keep washing the dirt away
I want to be like You, Jesus
A reflection of Your love
Help others to find their way
So they can bask in Your joy
Hidden beneath Your shadow
Lord I will follow You
Every step on the way
To my home in glory
Hidden beneath Your shadow

So many blessings I take for granted

Who is it that stands here gazing
I look across the span of time
With a thankful heart I just keep on praising
So many blessings I take for granted
The laughter of children
Rainy days and warm summer nights
Mother baking in her favorite apron
Food that's placed upon the table
Birds that fill the air
So many blessings I take for granted
Stars that shine in the night sky
Autumn leaves falling, giving way to spring
Caterpillars changing into butterflies
Music playing and people dancing
Campfires and waterfalls
Watching animals in the meadows
Quiet walks beside a gentle stream
Children playing in the snow
So many blessings I take for granted
Most of all it's the love that made it all possible
From where all blessings flow
They all come from God
This I'm sure you all know
In case you don't
These are just a few words to remind you

Have you forgotten the lonely hearts

Have you forgotten the lonely hearts
Those that huddle in doorways after dark
Who walk the streets in need of a friend
They hold up signs to get our attention
Do you see them
Are you willing to help
They're just hungry for a meal
Reach out and extend yourself
Be a helping hand
Have you forgotten the lonely hearts
Behind iron gates they lay
Some may never see or enjoy the freedom of the day
Or feel the embrace of their family
Nor receive a letter to brighten up their day
Don't forget them
Have you forgotten the lonely hearts
There are many who go without
While others have so much
We should all share so all can enjoy the blessing of the Lord
Don't be afraid to give up some time
To ease troubled hearts and minds
Be there for each and every one
So no one will feel forgotten or left behind

Going beyond expectations

To ease the pain in someone's life
That hope may be born in their hearts
Replacing frowns with smiles on their faces
We that know the Lord must show the love
Do more than what some believe is our share
All because we truly care
With no thought of our limitations
Driven by the Lord of creation
Who gives us purpose and motivation
Allowing us to accomplish an important goal
To help the well being of another soul
Going beyond expectations
When we allow ourselves to be directed by God
We are no longer part of the status quo
Being tossed around by our imperfection
Not trusting in the whims of man
This moves us beyond ordinary
Making some of us legendary
It's not who we think we are that defines us
God alone set the standard of what and who we should be
It is in His judgment we should trust
Doesn't it make more sense to follow perfection
Than the imperfections and flaws of man
When we are trying to go in an up-ward direction
Going beyond expectations
We will break from the box
We'll be more than normal
Because we dance to a different beat
Not only do we dance
But we run, jump, laugh and cry
We're just everyday people
The only difference is Who we serve
This keeps us **going beyond expectations**

Find Jesus

Are you tired of ups and downs
Tossing all through the night
Never closing your eyes
Worries constantly bombarding your mind
Is it peace you seek
Find Jesus
The Answer
Find Jesus
The Giver of peace
Is there a hole in your heart
Void of love
Empty and never been filled
Or were you broken down and love torn from you
Leaving a scar so very deep
Find Jesus
The Healer of wounds
Find Jesus
The Giver of undying love
He can restore what was lost
Or create a new flame of love
Why are you feeling sad
Can't find anything to smile about
This world is filled with many of God's wonders
Surely you can find joy in something
Well then what you need is a connection
A connection to The Most Highest
The One from where all blessings flow
It is through Him that we find joy
This allows us to enjoy what God has given through His Son
Peace, love and joy
When we **find Jesus**

Failure is part of life

We as people should not be so hard on ourselves
Because in this crazy mixed up world
Everybody falls sometimes
Failure is part of life
We all have to learn from our mistakes
Besides, if we never have hard times
If we have never been at wit's end
Then we would never know what God can do
Just how He can pull us through
No pain no gain
Failure is part of life
There are many things we may try to achieve
Hurdles and obstacles may bar our way
Because of the walls we encounter we feel like giving up
Did Jesus Christ die in vain?
I think not
Then there is no reason to walk in defeat
Victory has already been secured
Secured in every part of life
Through the blood that is our foundation
Only if we choose to allow His blood to cover us
With that said then we can get up
Try, try again and again
The trials in life are just character building
Failure is part of life

Sleep on my shoulder

My love, I'm at ease with you
So good to have you close to me
With the night wearing down
It's time to close our eyes
Sleep on my shoulder
Let's dance in a dream together
If it's God's will in the morning we will rise
Facing another day of love
I can't believe it sometimes
That it's you and me facing the challenges of life
What a wonderful joy it is
To have you as my wife
Up and down, round and round
I know life has its crazy moments
Then at the end of the day
Here we are relaxing in each other's arms
Laying aside our garments
As we prepare for another night together
With our eyes growing weary
Baby, go on and sleep
Sleep on my shoulder

Don't go out like you came in
Kicking and screaming

What will fussing and fighting bring
Why all the complaining
There's far too much hate in the world
We don't need all that confusion
Our hope is in the Lord above
To help us make it through
Don't go out like you came in
Kicking and screaming
Never having anything good to say
Always bringing somebody down
You use your tongue like a knife
Cutting people up from left to right
What you need is peace and love
Only found in the bosom of the Lord
Don't go out like you came in
Kicking and screaming
Never up, always down
No smile on your face
Always a frown
You check the grass on the other side
Never wanting to cut your own
Searching high and low for a drinking buddy
Or someone with some bad smoke
Misery loves company
So that old story goes
Sometimes you find yourself all alone
Because you have no peace
You have no joy
Which can only be found in the Lord
Don't go out like you came in
Kicking and screaming

Don't get caught up in the show

Things in life will come at you from all sides
They may look good on the outside
Never revealing its true nature
Under its cloak there are many faces
From the concealed to the obvious
In many ways it can be appealing
Don't get caught up in the show
Words can be so soft and gentle
Stirring up the soul
Pleasing to the eyes
With an underlying motive
Spinning a web like a spider
Catching many unaware
Smooth talkers
Lying lips
Don't get caught up in the show

Gary's Fried Chicken

Ingredients:
- 2 lbs of chicken (choose your pieces)
- Garlic powder
- Black pepper
- Season salt
- All purpose flour
- Grits
- Canola oil
- Large mixing bowl or large bag

Cooking instructions:
In large mixing bowl or bag add flour, grits and seasonings and mix well, and then set aside for later. Take care not to over season because you will use seasoning on the chicken as well. Wash chicken pieces and remove the skin. Lightly season them with the seasonings listed then roll chicken in the flour mixture. In a large skillet add canola oil and fry the chicken on med heat 20-30 minutes, until done.

Now enjoy with your favorite sides.

Options: Take 4 eggs and ½ cup of milk and beat well, and dip the chicken in the egg before rolling in the flour. Also, you can add crushed bran flakes to your flour mixture, or for extra crunch use grape nuts cereal.

Don't fall behind

In life there are many pitfalls
There are things that can and will hinder us
We cannot afford to live outside the protection of the Lord
Because it is His strength that sustains us
Which aids us in times of distress
Don't fall behind the line of defense
Where the enemy lies in wait to destroy us
Taking from us our will to stand
Leaving us with no dignity
Stripping us of our God-given rights
To live free from the grip of sin
Don't fall behind when the pace has been set
We are an army of blood-washed believers
Marching to the beat of love
With God as our Supreme Leader
Who watches over us and provides for us
Without Him we will fall behind
Don't fall behind

Don't forget the sacrifice

Don't forget the sacrifice
The one Jesus paid for us
He gave us a chance to be free
Free from the penalty that lies beyond the grave
Crushing forever the lie that the devil brought to us
In his attempt to break our spirit
Don't forget the sacrifice
That the almighty God has done
What would you give for your loved ones
Would you give up your son
For someone you don't know
Let him die and shed his blood
For strangers of love
Don't forget the sacrifice
Too great a price has been paid
Motivated by the greatest love of all
The door has been opened to a wonderful life
Mercy and grace we have received
It's up to us
To take that gift of life
Share it with as many that will listen
The time is shorter than we think
Satan wants our souls
We can stand and fight
Or give in to his control
We have the weapon
The power is in the blood
Don't forget the sacrifice

Did you listen

When He called your name
In the middle of the night
Did you hear that voice in your ear
Stand still so you can hear and know that He is God
Did you listen to what He has to say
Did you listen
To that painful voice of hunger
Can you hear them crying
Don't close your ears
Can't you hear Him saying "feed the hungry
Take care of those who are sick
Share your many blessings with the less fortunate ones
Visit those locked behind walls of concrete and steel
Help the lost to find their way"
Did you listen
There's a lot of work to be done
Did you listen
When that cry for help came ringing through your ears
Did you help that one in distress
Or say you couldn't get involved
Did you listen when He said the battle is not ours
It's not against flesh and blood
The battle is with principalities
Beware of wolves in sheep's clothing
Like a lion waiting in the darkness
To steal your soul
Did you listen

Deep inside my secret place

When the things outside myself
Begin to wear me down
There's a place where I can go
To escape the mundane drags of life
A place of solitude
Deep inside my secret place
Where I can talk with God above
In that place I'm at peace as I connect with God
Telling Him just what's on my mind
When no one else will listen
He hears me when I call
I praise Him through it all
He's my Lord and Savior
Deep inside my secret place
I find joy and comfort there
His peace and love surrounds me
I'm so glad He's always near
He chastises me when I'm wrong
Because He loves me I keep holding on
Deep inside my secret place
No one can hurt me there
It's guarded by the hands of God
The One Who never sleeps and always cares
If you feel somewhat like me
And you need a place to be free
There's a place you can go
On your knees beside your bed or anywhere at all
In your secret place
There you can pray
Just like me
Deep inside my secret place

Dead weight

Dead weight
Who wants it?
It's nothing but excess baggage
Dead weight
Who needs it?
Always in the way
If you don't free yourself from it
Your life will be ruined
Dead weight
Do you dream of something or somewhere you want to go?
You will never reach that goal
Dragging that dead weight behind you
You must change your thinking
Elevate your mind
You can't make it on your own
Reach out and call on the Divine
Dead weight
It's a show stopper
Never means you any good
It can change your attitude
Make you feel you're good for nothing
It will rob you of your joy
Rearrange the deepest parts of you
Tear down your confidence
Take without giving anything back
The words "I can do all things"
Seem to fade from your lips
That's what it does
Dead weight
It's low self esteem
Jealousy
Envy
Hatred and holding unforgiveness in your heart
Only doing for yourself and nobody else
Dead weight will make you a lonely person
Nobody wants it around
Dead weight

Daughters of purpose

Today and everyday of your life you must be strong
Not in your own strength
But in the One who aids your cause
In life many will sit back and watch how you stand
So are you standing like a super human?
Or are you keeping it real?
You cry, you hurt and you have flaws
Yet in your weakness you can stand
Because of the love He has for you
This mission field is a long journey
You will be successful on that road to glory
Because you have a desire to do God's will
There will be joy in the hearts of many
A wonderful smile on the face of a lost one
Because of your determination and the time you took to care
Lives will be changed by the Master that lives in you
Children, husbands and wives, mothers and fathers
Many others as well who fall under your sphere of influence
With Christ you will live up to the challenge
I wonder do you know who you are with your imperfect self
That can do big things with perfection that inhabits your soul
Look at you standing in the midst of a storm
You have become a shoulder for someone to lean on
You are a child of The Most High
Full of compassion
Drawing your strength from the well of life
The source of living water
You are the **Daughter of purpose**

Come on sinners, come on

His arms are open wide
Just waiting to receive you
Why base your life on a whim or a chance
The ground you are standing on is shaky
Come on, trust in God above
The One who has so much love
Come on sinners, come on
There's more in store for you
Beyond your wildest dreams
Just come and see
You don't want to be out there on that limb
When it breaks one day what will you do
Don't take that chance
Stand on that firm foundation
Where there is more room than you need
Try the Lord for yourself
Come on sinners, come on

Come and pray

When you feel you can't find your way
And love is on the outs
Come and pray
Bills are piling up too high
You have more month than money
Come and pray
Get down on your knees
Remember the five thousand that were fed
Just give thanks for what you have
Jesus can do the impossible
Come and pray
Is your body racked with pain
Has your child lost his way
Kneel before the mighty hand of God
There is nothing too hard for Him
Come and pray
You're at the lowest point in your life
From the ground you can see a lot clearer
You've been broken into a million pieces
Your heart is aching
Tears they just keep on falling
Through times like these
Close your eyes and see Him
Come and pray
God will never leave you
Keep the faith and never give up
Come and pray
He will hear and deliver
When your strength seems to fail you
Trust in Him and He will carry you
He's a never failing God
Come and pray

Beyond the pain

I know it hurts you deep down inside
You feel like you're drowning and in need of air
Many words have been shared
That can lead you from your despair
So in your decision making choose wisely
You must look **beyond the pain**
I know it may seem hard
That's only because you're in the way
You must look at your dilemma through the eyes of Jesus
Then remember the cross
He had to endure and look **beyond the pain**
At all the souls that would be saved
Now don't think He didn't have doubts about it
He was dressed in human flesh
Cried, ate, slept, hurt and felt just like you
There's a much bigger picture than His will
It's the will of the Father that the family survives
You are part of that family if you choose
Choose to see that greater picture
Which could take a lifetime, but the rewards are eternal
Like Nehemiah said, the joy of the lord is your strength
You can do it, just look **beyond the pain**
Paul said we find joy in our tribulations
That means the devil is at work and you're being tested
Hold on, my brother, and look **beyond the pain**

From your loving brother
Gary and the Lord Jesus Christ

Because of You I can see my tomorrow

The past is behind me
I can't go back
Too much pain and misery
I must keep my eyes on the prize
Which is ahead of me
My mind is clear
It feels so good to breathe
Because of You I can see my tomorrow
We all have some bad days
That's part of living down here
It's about how we face them
Do I lie down
Do I stand up on my feet
If it's on my knees I go
Am I there to pray
To the One Who has it all
Because of You I can see my tomorrow
To be clean on the inside
Makes everything on the outside better
There will be some hills in my life
Some valleys to go through
That's alright as long as I'm wrapped up in You
Because of You I can see my tomorrow

As we become one

Love will be our guide
Many trials we will face
But never alone
We will taste the bitter with the sweet
Endure the test of time
God, He will keep us
As we cherish Him above all
As we become one
Our lives blending together
Within the Glory of Christ
Pledging our lives
To have and to hold
Until heaven's gate
What a journey this will be
As we become one

Are you a reflection of His love?

Are you a reflection of His love?
Do you mirror the character of Who He is?
Can you deny yourself when love calls?
Calls you to stand in the gap for someone who can't
Can you pick up the pieces of someone's life?
Then put them back together again?
Can you feed the hungry and put clothes on the backs of those
without?
Would you put your life on the line for someone you don't know?
Will you take the message of hope to the world?
Are you a person without sin?
Can you love someone like Jesus loves?
Now if you answered yes to these questions
Then you are truly a gem
The body of Christ has many members
Jesus being totally God and totally human
With that human body He did not sin
A perfect being in a flawed body
Are you a reflection of His love?
Apart we will not achieve that love He inspired
Together we can fulfill love's great desire
Only when we stand as one
We can be a reflection of His love

A mother's hope

Tears are falling from her eyes
Sad and joyful at the same time
Tangled and mixed they fall
Somberly she looks to heaven
Praying to Jesus for her son
With words on her lips
"I haven't seem him in so long
Where I can hold him
Kiss him on the cheek
Tell him mother knows"
She cries to Jesus as she kneels before Him
The only One Who can make sense of it all
Comfort my heart, dear sweet Lord
You're **a mother's hope**
I trust You with my life
I'm calling on You, Jesus
Not for me, but for my son
Who is longing to be free
He is locked away
Looking for the light of day
Humbly I pray
Some nights prostrate on the floor I lay
You're **a mother's hope**
Just watch over him
Guard his heart
So when he comes to my arms again
The love of You, Jesus, all over him
Thank You, Jesus
You're **a mother's hope!**

When Your work in me is done I will slip away

So much work to be done
There are many lives that must be touched
Hearts are aching and yearning for love
Take this vessel, use me for Your glory
Shape me with Your mighty hand
Refine my life, fill me with Your Spirit
So my life will reflect Your love
When Your work in me is done I will slip away
Allow me to be Your representative
So much to do
With little time to do it
I'm only a vapor fading with time
Like a tender green leaf that has served its purpose
Soon to whither and fall from the branches
To adorn the ground with many others
Serving now a different purpose
A memory that points to the future
When Your work in me is done I will slip away
Until then help me to be all that You want me to be
So others will see and be moved by Your Spirit
To walk beyond the boundaries of this earth
As they too reach out to others
Moved and used by Your Spirit
Thank You, Jesus

What's up people

What's up people
Jesus loves you
Gave His life just to save you
On that cross He laid it down so plain
You better check your life and check it well
Or you may miss the best of life
People, people
Don't you worry
I know you've heard that living story
How Jesus paid a price no one could pay
You better listen and listen well
He is soon to come again
With all power in His hands
Lonely people
Stop your crying
You don't have to keep complaining
You can do something about your life
Just look to Jesus, He's the answer you need
He can mend broken hearts and lift your soul
You better hear me, and hear me well
We can't make it without Jesus
Hateful people
Stop all that hating
There is a day of reckoning coming
Too many children growing up without fathers
Mother's eyes swollen and red
She cries for the loss of a child
Innocent blood flowing in our streets
Caught in the crossfire of hateful people
You better heed this warning and heed it well
No evil will prevail
Saith the Lord
What's up people

What is poetry?

Is it the written expression of the thoughts of the mind?
With pen in hand a writer attempts to capture those things on paper
Is it the melody of the heart?
The melody one makes because of the joys and pains of life?
As we listen to the voice of a brilliant singer
The words seem to come alive
Allowing us to identify with the very essence of its meaning
Bringing laughter or tears falling from our eyes
What is poetry?
Is it a painter laying on canvas the beauties of life?
Maybe it's the birds that soar with grace
As they fill God's blue skies
What is poetry?
It's anything and everything
It's what the eyes can see
The heart can feel
It's a sound your ears may hear
It's a song or the spoken word
It's a story expressed in many different ways
The end of it all will lead us to the source
Where true poetry resides
In the mind of God

We all will go together

Let me tell you all something
I want it to marinate deep down inside of you
Not everyone that says "Yes, Lord" will sit on clouds of joy
Some have made their beds on brimstones
They disregard the Blood that atones
One thing I know
We all will go together
To one place or the other
Don't be blind to the light of Love
So much has been given to help us find our way
You see Love cared so much
He stepped down from the realm above
Tell me who are you going to trust
Do you want His divine touch
Or is it the things of this world you will continue to clutch
We all will go together
Where is your final resting place
They say where your heart is so is your home
We must be abased
To help those that wear sin like a garment
So that they too can receive God's loving grace
Color and creed has no relevance
We all will go together
To be caught up in the clouds
Or to fiery punishment we will fall
We have a choice
Heed God's warning
Or live with the consequence

Until we learn we are not free

When things in life seem so difficult
Like a thorn in your side
Nagging you like a splinter under your skin
Remember, when handling wood, gloves will help
Until we learn we are not free
When eyes red from crying and you're feeling blue
There's a reason for all the pain
Something needs to change
You must come to grips with yourself
I know it's hard sometimes
Salty residue on your lips as your tears fall
Things are out of place
God says examine yourself
Looking in the mirror is hard to do
For the reflection we see is us
This is where we need to start if we want to change
Until we learn we are not free
Man was not created to live in bondage
God made us free spirits
We are supposed to enjoy the blessings of the Lord
But the lower form took advantage of our innocence
Bringing greed and selfishness into our lives
This now requires a savior to set us free
There is joy in being free if we choose to take it
Until we learn we are not free

The words escape me sometimes

Sometimes I just don't know what to say
My heart is filled with gratitude
Because You are there for me
Your love goes far beyond my fault
As often as I complain
And those wrong things that consumed my life
Only You could bring me out
So many thoughts run through my head
How do I say thank You
The words escape me sometimes
To put in words what You have done for me
I can't seem to find them
There are no words in man's vocabulary
That can adequately describe
Or even come close to the joy that envelopes my heart
All I know is to be free from the pain
Pain that hurts those I love
As long as I live
I could never repay what it means to me
You have saved my life
So as I struggle to find the words
I just want to say to the best of my ability
Thank You

Take my heart

Baby, I have something for you
Something that only you can take
It's the love that I possess inside
Come **take my heart**
It is yours, my love
Because you are so close to me
You create joy in so many ways
Kissing all my blues away
When I'm in your arms I feel at ease
Other then God above its you I want to please
Take my heart
You know it's yours, baby
No one else can do for me like you
You are the sweetness on my lips
Like sweet wine I can't stop with one sip
I'm totally wrapped up in you
Take my heart
Enjoy yourself
Relax and bathe in my endless love
Imperfect but for real
Take my heart

Strengthened by hard times

Everyday somebody is going through it
Late at night someone is laying their head down in tears
Shaken by some kind of tragedy
How do we deal with the pain?
Do we sit back and sing a sad refrain?
Feeling sorry for our selves
We have to learn through our mistakes
Stand up when the going gets ruff
Be confident and know we will make it
We are **strengthened by hard times**
Not everyone is born into wealth
Working hard for what you have brings satisfaction
You see, when you go through the fire
It's like metal being forged
Heated and bended until it takes on the shape intended
You can't have a diamond without tremendous pressure
Life has its way of preparing us for the fight
Strengthened by hard times
Why is the endurance of pain necessary?
Are we not just ordinary?
I believe that the answer is in the Voice that is calling
If you listen you will hear Him say
"Be strong and hang on"
It's going to get better after while
You're going through so you can tell others
So they can tell others
That troubles don't last always
Strengthened by hard times
It will get us ready for glory
To walk in the halls of the King
Where hard times will be no more
Peace and joy are reigning forever
So until then just remember
We are **strengthened by hard times**
This leads to good times

Somebody's child

What is this world coming to?
When a child can go unnoticed
A little mind left to fend for its own
Wandering outside alone
They could be yours
But it's **somebody's child**
Somebody's child has tears in their eyes
Poverty stricken, on a bed of straw they lie
Food is something hard to come by
While some bask in abundance
They're not willing to share
Tell me why
I believe you know
Somebody's child has a dream
To live in a world with no more wars
Where peace and love defines us all
Joy is worn like a garment
A land where there is plenty for everyone
Where man is no longer ruled by greed and lust
That place where we can truly say
In God we trust
Somebody's child needs to know that they are loved
In some cases it's not in the home
That's where we all can step up
Be a big brother or sister
Maybe a mother or a father
Someone who's just willing to love
Someone in need of love
Maybe this is you
Because we all are
Somebody's child

So many memories

Across the span of time
Through out the time man is allotted
There will be moments to reflect on
So many memories
Where does one start in the examination of one's life?
Maybe it's thinking back to a time of innocence
When we were children
Seeing the world as a wonderful place
Capturing the beauty of life with eyes so big and bright
Locking those pretty pictures in the recesses of our minds
Like a painter's brush strokes across the canvas
Preserving the beauty that they see
Windows to the past
So many memories
Looking back can be good at times
Allowing us to see how far we have come
Through times of pain and heartache
Yes, there were struggles and times of joy
But we have found our way
The past reveals to us in the present
Things we need to correct for the future
So that there will be memories
Memories of a time that has faded into yesterday
This will point the way for those yet to come
Families sitting beside the fireplaces
Going through picture albums and telling the stories
Little children sitting on grandpa's knee
As he fills their ears with stories of the family
So many memories
Keep it going and let us learn from the past
So that our children's children will have a future
As they learn and pass it on
So many memories

Nothing but the grace of God

Nothing but the grace of God
That allows me to be here
Whether I believe or not
He's the writer of the script
Changing characters at His discretion
Allowing things to come into my life
Good or bad to improve my character
Nothing but the grace of God
Who cares so much for me
I'm just clay in the Potter's hands
Molding me, shaping me
I just have to listen and bend to his will
If He's not pleased with me
Back in the oven I go
Until I can't go in no more
To wind up in the garage bin
Or to be placed up on the shelf
Noting but the grace of God
Can turn bad into good
It could have been different for me
One wrong turn, there's poverty
It could have been me sleeping in alleyways
Or traveling somewhere far
Maybe even sitting behind bars
In life it's all about choices we make
As God tries to direct our path
Without a forceful hand
Nothing but the grace of God
That allows us to choose
He is love

No matter what it looks like
It will turn around

No matter what it looks like
It will turn around
No matter what it feels like
It will be alright
Walls may fall around me
The enemy may try to break me down
Try to steal my joy and hope
That's when I sing to myself
Songs of praise to the Lord above
Down on bended knees I pray
Looking back to Calvary
Remembering what Jesus done for me
The grave couldn't hold Him
So why should I be discouraged
Walls can be rebuilt
Broken hearts can be mended
It's all about holding on
To the One Who holds it all
No matter what it looks like
It will turn around
No matter how hard things may seem
There's a better day on the horizon
It's all about believing in His Holy Name
Trusting in Him through all the pain
Stand! When that seems so hard
Until the end of the road
No matter what it looks like
It will turn around

More than a lucky chance

Every now and then true love is found
Puts a smile on your face
Fills your heart with laughter
No need to hide who you are
It's like being on a cloud drifting free
It's more than a lucky chance
A four leaf clover will never do
To find a love that's true
Nothing happens by chance
No horse shoes or a rabbit's foot
Wishbones or Tarot cards
Can ever lead you to true love
Only God above can direct love that is true
Now if you want to believe in things so vague
Putting your trust in things that do not matter
Go right ahead
But for me
It's more than a lucky chance

Many years
Many tears

Many years
Many tears
We have weathered many storms
Tears of joy
Tears of pain
If it's God's will we will share many more
I have given you my love
With all of its faults
My love, you deserve much more than what I have to give
There's no material thing that can convey what I really feel
So with these words I offer the inside of me
A small consolation for all the years
Hoping for more joy, trust and love
As we look forward to another twenty years
Nothing can please me more than your smiling face
To be wrapped up tight in your embrace
Second only to the Lord above
Many years
Many tears

It only gets better from here
Happy anniversary

Keep holding His hand

I feel sometimes like giving up
But I know I must **keep holding His hand**
He will never fail me
I know I'm going to make it
Because of Jesus I can see my way
It may look dark and gloomy
Over mountains and through valleys I will go
As long as I **keep holding His hand**
It's going to be alright
You know when things are going good
That's when I should have stood strong
Not in my own strength
But in the power of the Lord
I took Him for granted
When I should have humbled myself
Now I'm crying
Humility is a hard thing when you're not prepared
So like David I cry
Make my heart like You want it, Lord
Restore Your peace and joy within me
I love You, my sweet Lord
I'm going to **keep holding Your hand**
That's the only thing that will get me through
I'll keep holding His hand

It's been done before

There is nothing new
It's been done before
Dreamers have always dreamed
Lovers continue to love
War spills innocent blood
Peacemakers keep on trying
It's been done before
From mothers children are born
We watch them grow into someone we adore
A father gives his blessing
To a child who learns to soar
Leaving to begin a life all their own
Time keeps on moving
Lives are forever changing
There is nothing God is not aware of
It's been done before
Waves breaking along the seashore
Crashing upon the rocks you can hear the roar
People gazing into the night sky
Always asking the question "why?"
Searching for the answers
To some things we will never find
As this world keeps on turning
There are things not for us
They are only for The Divine
But we keep on trying
It's been done before

Is it really Christmas or just another holiday?

Winter time is here again
It's a favorite time of the year
There will be snow on rooftops
Some will see rainy days and nights
Streets will be filled with autumn leaves
Throughout many neighborhoods
Mornings will be cold and frosty
As another year comes to an end
Cities dressed in a very festive style
Lights hanging from the trees
In a variety of colors
Many homes will be decked out as well
All in preparation for Christmas morning
To celebrate the birth of the King
The day will bring together family and friends
Tables will be filled with delicious delights
It will be cold outside
So snug like a bug in a rug
Many will warm themselves by the holiday fire
Christmas morning will bring laughter
Children's eyes will sparkle
As they rip and tear at their presents
Stockings hanging all around
Loaded with holiday cheer
Is it really Christmas or just another holiday?
Unfortunately not everyone will find that Christmas cheer
No warm beds or cozy fires
No presents under the trees
No hot meals or delicious delights
I say again
Is it really Christmas or just another holiday?

In the morning love will win

In the morning love will win
Love will get you through
In the morning love will overshadow your faults
It will lead you through troubled times
Love will take care of your heart
By surrendering to its awesome power
Then you'll know how wonderful it is
Love will allow you to understand
Love will help you listen to someone's heart
Because everyone wants to be heard
In the morning you can smell the dew that covers the ground
The day has a fresh new start
That's what love will do
For me and for you
In the morning yesterday has faded into the past
A new day has dawned
With a life all its own
With new challenges for that day
Facing a world of wonders ahead
We all suffer from the same things in life
Being manipulated by things that do not matter
But when we tap in to the source
Where true love lies
Deep inside the heart and mind of God
We can overcome any obstacle
In the morning love will win

I'll never let You go

Through all my ups and downs
I will keep on holding Your hand
As You hold mine
Through my temptations and trials
I'll never let You go
Keep on holding me up, Lord
When I'm weak give me the strength to carry on
Keep on lifting me as I soar higher
Your love is so good to me
I'll never let You go
You're the answer to every question I every had
Music of You Lord fills my soul
In sad times it's Your joy that gets me by
In You I find peace to calm my raging spirit
Without You there is no me
I'll never let You go
It's Your love I know that sustains me
I should try everyday to emulate Your love
Allow it to penetrate my heart
So I can be used by You in this life
A tool to help others to find the way
Until You call me home
I love You Lord
I'll never let You go

If I don't have time

If I don't have time to kiss you and say goodbye
Before I close my eyes
If I don't have time to hold you one last time
I want you to know I love you
My wife and sister and friend
We will meet again in the house of the Lord

If I don't have time to say much more to you
To kiss you, hold you, my children
Be strong, for I'm not out of your life
I'm closer than a memory
So take my words to your heart
I want to see you again
When we dance at the foot of God's throne
So many things I want to say and share
All my hopes and dreams
I can't think of anything more precious
Than the thoughts from my heart
So **if I don't have time**
Remember I love you

I was so close but I didn't knock

I remember when I was down and I didn't know Jesus
Lost and on my own
Then someone told me I can make it through
If I believe in Jesus who I cannot see
The door was right there in front of me
I was so close but I didn't knock
A hand of love reached out to me
I was so blind
Seems like a veil was over my eyes
Doing my own thing
Bound by the pleasures of this world
Nevertheless in my heart I was longing to be free
I was so close but I didn't knock
There was a time that I cried
Until my eyes turned red
Pain deep in my heart
As I laid there in my bed
I felt there was no one to rescue me
But I kept hearing words from my friends
"Get to know Jesus and new life will begin"
I was so close but I didn't knock
Then one day I knocked on that door
All my cares seemed to drift away
Now I know what I've been missing
I'm free in the midst of my trials
I have peace in the middle of chaos
Joy beyond my pain
Now I am saved

I was made to praise You

I was made to praise You
With everything that's in me
I was made to praise You
Like the mountains and the trees
From a small gentle brook
To the sound of a raging river
Everything in nature praises Your Name
I was made to praise You
Just like all Your wonders that dance before our eyes
The seasons change by Your design
Winter, spring, summer, fall
Snow flakes glistening across the ground
Clouds gather overhead to water the earth
New life springs into action to adorn the land
Sunny days and the nights are warm
With many gazing into the star filled night
Then an autumn leaf falls, singing Your praise
Like everything around me
I was made to praise You
Jesus

I understand why He died for me

So I could be totally free
When I stand in the midst of a storm
The pains of life will surely come
My integrity will be tested
Through it all I am not alone
It's through His strength that I can make it
Of my own I cannot boast
I'm nothing without Him
To think otherwise is a mistake
I understand why He died for me
He did something I could not do
Paying a price for me and this world of sin
Stepping down from His divine post
To live with us and give hope
Showing me the strength of love
By demonstrating the power of humility
He's indeed the King of kings
The Lord of lords
I understand why He died for me

You make my heart sing

I just want to say
You make my heart sing
Every time I think of You, Lord
My heart sings
So good to know You invade my thoughts
There's a melody of freedom in my soul
I can't hold it inside of me
I must tell the world
Tell them all about You
Just how **You make my heart sing**
Every time I dream about You
My heart sings
So much joy inhabits my soul
You are with me while I sleep
You're a Guardian
Watching over me
I'm so glad You are there for me
There is no moment I am alone
You make my heart sing
It doesn't matter where I go
Or the changes I go through
You are always there
You are in my dreams and every waking moment
You paid the price for my salvation
I will always lift Your Name
Even after my last breath in this life
You make my heart sing

You have eyes to see
Ears to hear

Take your hands from your eyes
So you can see where you're going
Why would anyone want to walk in the dark
It's much better in the light
Open your ears so you can hear
God's message ringing clear
You have eyes to see, ears to hear
Why not use what God has given
To see injustice and make a difference
To hear a cry for help
In a sea of many voices
You have eyes to see, ears to hear
What good is your sight
When you have blinders on
What about your ears when you don't want to listen
To a message of love given over two thousand years ago
Nothing in life has really changed
Things are still the same
People see what they want
They hear without listening
But through it all many are still in the hunt
God's message will prevail
From now and to the end of our time
Remember you can open your ears
From your eyes you can remove the veil
You have eyes to see, ears to hear

Where do we go from here

People come in many shapes and colors
Sometimes anger grips the heart
Angry for nothing
Manipulated by something
To keep us at each other's throats
Never stopping to realize
We are all headed for the ground
Ashes to ashes
Dust to dust
This is something that is common to all
But before we fall
Let's try to change our course
Where do we go from here
The blood of a child stains the ground
Innocence is crying out
Open your ears so you can hear
The cries that fill our streets
Open your eyes so you can see
The devastation and the misery
The world is changing
Into what I don't know
What ever it will be
It's up to us
We should heed the words of God
In Whom we should trust
Or lie down and let the end be worse than the beginning
Where do we go from here

Raindrops from heaven

I enjoy basking in the sun
On a warm summer's day
Walking with my lady as we watch the sunset
Laying on a blanket on a grassy hillside
Gazing into the heavens on a starry night
So wonderful to be alive
God has so many wonders
Gentlemen, have you ever walked with your baby in the rain
Letting the **raindrops from heaven** fall on your faces?
It's so good when you're in love
Like two children playing under the stars above
Kisses so sweet, oh how good it tastes
Raindrops from heaven
They come down in many forms and shapes
It's the food we eat
The garments that we wear to cover our bodies
Houses and cars and the lights that twinkle in the night
People, animals, places and things
Every good thing you can imagine
That list goes on and on
Raindrops from heaven
They are the blessing that God has given
My family and friends
The woman that I love
Most of all it's His love
Which comes to us from the rays of the Son
Jesus

America I think you're great
But you forgot something

America let me bend your ears for a moment
I know that you were a problem child
Your mother experienced much pain at your birth
But here you are at God's placement
Yes you struggle with your identity
To live up to your sounding greed
You have been inspired by Biblical accounts
Evident on the parchments that lies behind glass
The Declaration of Independence
The United States Constitution and the Bill on Rights
Behind glass, yes things are fragile
America I think you're great
But you forgot something
It's more than paper that makes a nation
Show us you care by your leadership
Great leaders are inspired by God
Motivated to show compassion
With genuine concern for the hearts of the people
America I think you're great
But you forgot something
I guess I'm just thinking out loud
Our children are being victimized by program cuts
Tell me what good are all those rockets
We don't want to hear about some one walking in space
If you could walk the unkind streets
Go to the places our children play
Not just in the upscale communities
But in the places many have forgotten
Where pain and suffering, yes even death is a struggle
We must all rise up
As one people under God
To help this nation live out the standards we have set
So no one will be left behind
America I think you're great
But you forgot something

Keep in touch with the Master

How do I get the best out of life?
Where do I find the answers?
In who's arms do I long to be?
For me there is only One
I need to **keep in touch with the Master**
In Him I have all that I need
Peace, love and joy
Without these things life doesn't mean a thing
My relationships with family and friends
Could never reach the height of true fulfillment
Because everything that is good comes from the Lord
I need to **keep in touch with the Master**
Yes I could try to love you on my own
But my love, it's not good enough
I will disappoint you
It is not my intention to do so
It's just that I'm wrapped up in flesh like you
How can I stand with pain gripping my heart
What I need to keep me strong
I can't find it in the eyes of man
That's why I cry out to Him
I need to **keep in touch with the Master**
He's the one who keeps me in all of my trials
When my life doesn't measure up
I may sit on my bedside and cry awhile
Then on my knees I humble myself
I can only do this with His love guiding me
That's why I need to **keep in touch with the Master**

What is it that surrounds your heart

In the morning if you see another day
What will be on your mind
Will you think about all the people
Who feel they've been left behind
Can you show a hearty welcome
For some one you've never known
What is it that surrounds your heart
Is it love or is it something else
Do you have peace in your life
Knowing that some one you past on the street
May not have enough to eat
In church you raise your hands in praise
You thank God for the joy inside your heart
While people everyday are lost in a maze
Trapped in a rat race
With so much pain written on their face
They want to get out
But it seems they have been shutout
On their knees they cry and shout
All they need is a hand
What is it that surrounds your heart

Unkind streets

What's happening to this world
There are places you just don't go after dark
I wonder if we will ever hold that pearl
Will the hands of man ever find that spark
To stand against all the odds
Take back the ground that was promised
By the all loving and mighty God
If we stand on His principles
We don't have to be afraid of these **unkind streets**
Where babies come up missing
Can you feel the mothers and their heartbeats
Too much innocent blood, we must stop the bleeding
Allow God to work in our hearts
So we can walk in the light of love
There is nothing to fear on the **unkind street**
When we walk in the power of the Lord
We all will make that transformation
The only thing that evil can do is speed up the process
But there will be a day of reckoning
Some will then walk with angels
Others will feel the heat of God's anger
Then let's get busy and take back the **unkind streets**

Momma said don't point

How can you point your finger at me
I'm just like you
With my own set of problems
I'm not perfect and nether are you
We should not throw stones
Glass is fragile
Have you ever thrown a pebble in a pond
Did you watch the ripples
See life operates the same way
When we throw rocks houses crumble
People lives are forever changed
The screams, the pain in hurting hearts
Are the sounds of breaking glass
Why can't we just let the waters be smooth
Let God be the one to judge us
Heaven or hell we can't put anyone in
Instead of pointing out the faults in others
Why can't we help one another
True love is an action word
It's something that should be worn outward
We all struggle in life
Don't you think we should show more love
Then maybe, just maybe things could be different
Enough with the finger pointing
Momma said don't point

Lord guide my direction

Down on my knees with tears in my eyes
I feel like I'm on a far away journey
On a ship that has been capsized
Wash ashore by giant waves
All I can do is reach out to the one who saves
Lord guide my direction
It's a very lonely place to be isolated
Watch over me until I find my destination
It's hard and I feel so jaded
I want to stop now and rest awhile
Sometimes the grass looks greener on the other side
Never thinking that the grass over there needs cutting too
Lord guide my direction
It can get difficult at times
Walking through the valley of temptation
So many things running through my mind
But you said put on the whole armor
Then walk right behind you
You would be my fortress of defense
When I'm falling, feeling like I can't stand
You will be there to pick me up
When I call your name
Lord guide my direction

No time to rest

People all over are dying
Mothers are crying
A child grows up and marches off to war
The battle is raging on
Evil never takes a holiday
We must then continue the fight
No time to rest
Drugs are polluting the land
Destroying anyone it can
Pulling down so many families
Not enough care to go on their knees
The valiant must keep on praying
That God will soon intervene
Until that day comes
No time to rest
What is the future going to be for our children
Are we going to leave them chaos and confusion
Instead of the tools to defeat the enemy
If we dance to the beat of the Holy drums
We have an army of angels to aid our cause
So let's fight until the fight is done
No time to rest
There are to many lives at stake
So what we must do we must do it now
The future is not a guaranty
Jesus can return at any time
We need to keep that thought on our minds
Then went we make it to the other side
He said he will wipe all tears from our eyes
In that place then we can rest
Until then, there is **No time to rest**

Silent pains

Deep within the confines of my mind
I struggle; I wrestle with things that I don't understand
Painful memories haunting me
I know where true freedom lies
Yet it's hard to reach out
To free myself from my **silent pains**
I must find a way to unshackle myself
It's not just me that is affected
There are those around me that I love
That somehow is drifting from me
Yes it's a dilemma that I face
Silent pains
Silently killing the spirit that God has given
Help me, I cry to you Lord
I really don't know how to connect with you
Help me find myself in you
I know I can't break free from this silent killer
Without your hands of deliverance
Help me to find my way
Until then I will
I truly must deal
With these things that are derailing me
Pulling me into an abyss
Taking me places I do not want to go
I know there is a better way
To escape these **silent pains**

Moonlight madness

Can't you feel it in the air
The days are longer
Nights are getting warmer
Spring time weather
Moving people closer together
We are headed for some starry nights
Midnight walks in the moonlight
Paddleboats on the water that is smooth as glass
Jazzy music soothing our ears
We dock the boat to lie out on the grass
Moonlight madness
It is taking over
I can see it in your eyes
What a wonderful way to in the day
Lying here gazing into God's glory
So many wonderful things to do
Life is one great big turn on
With most on it for free
Moonlight madness
Can't you feel all the laughter
So much joy gripping the hearts
It's not just spring and summer
I look forward to everyday God has given
The moon is up there
Shinning down in winter and fall
It's just good to be on God's green earth
Thank you Lord
For the **moonlight madness**

Children

Children are our future
Do you have any of your own
A mother is somewhere crying
Standing by just helpless
As her child dies in her arms
Through the night she's so restless
Worried about her other little ones
Can't you see your arms reaching
Making a difference in the lives of so many
Don't you know it's the right thing to do
We are all in this together
You and me we are all **Children**
Under the watchful eyes of God
Children, yes the **children**
So many of them are falling
All around the world
I know you can feel the pain
Can't you hear their voices
It's not just a sad refrain
In their eyes you can see the hope
As we struggle in the mist of evil
So many lives I know will be lost
But there are so many victories
So just keep on fighting
For the **children** of the world
Remember Jesus is watching

I speak because of Love

There are so many things that I want to share with you
I thank God for the ability to articulate words
That I may be able to touch your heart with mine
I speak because of Love
My life in this world is not a perfected one
It's just a simple life that I live
Filled with ups and downs
Pains and laughter I wear them on my face
Tears fall from my eyes to the ground
Strength is in weakness and it sets its own pace
Maybe something I say can give some encouragement
I speak because of Love
Love takes care of my heart
I'm here to tell you how much Love means to me
Without it I'm just blowing in the wind
I need Love so I can get that message across
When I hurt I call out to Love
Then Love responds to me
I can feel it and I know I'm not lost
He speaks to me
Motivates me when I need motivation
He calms my raging spirit
Soothes my troubled mind
Lets me know everything will work out fine
I speak because of Love
Love is all we need to make it through
So give it a try
Don't let it get past your life
I speak because of Love

Well here we are at the end of the journey; I hope you have had an enjoyable experience. It has been my joy to have been your guide on this wonderful adventure of love. I want to leave you with these final thoughts: how do we as God-fearing people deal with a world of controversy? Is it by compromising? I think not, but we compromise everyday in some form. How do we do this, you may be asking yourself. It's very simple really: we do it more often than we think, by doing things that go against our goals or plans we set for ourselves. We also do it when it comes to our morals and values, and this list goes on and on.

Here are a few examples: the food we eat everyday, the cars we drive, the house we live in and the clothes on our backs – we compromise these things everyday. We also compromise ourselves in so many ways. We buy a lot of things we don't need, we live way above our means, which causes a whole lot of other problems. And that's not all. Look at the time we spend with family and friends, and the way we spend our time. You get the point, I hope. You see, there are so many ways to compromise, and we do it without even knowing or thinking about it. Some compromising is a good thing, but we must be careful, because it can cause controversy in our lives and erode our integrity.

What, then, does this mean for us? Well, I believe to live out our lives to its full potential we must evaluate where and what we want out of life. The where is how and where we fit into the grand scheme of things. To understand this speaks to the heart of our value system. Are we here by divine conception or by a series of accidental happenings? Now if we are here by the handy work of God, which I believe, then there is a prescribed and clear direction that God would have us to conduct our lives. With divine intervention God has provided us with a set of rules to follow, which will help us to reach our potential. Now on the other hand, if we are here by accident, then our choices are limited, and it doesn't really matter what we do or think, because everyone would be going in opposite directions.

With so many individual thought patterns, and without a true direction, the only outcome would be total chaos. With no one willing to follow anyone the world will be a terrible place full of pain, but I believe the world would be over as we know it. People with no direction and left to themselves will destroy themselves.

Now I know that was a mouthful, but we are at an end, and there is still one thing yet to be said which I feel would benefit not only you and I, but our children as we prepare them for times to come. The lesson is clear; we must envision Godly things that bring about a positive attitude to help us obtain a peaceful and loving disposition in the now, which will set us up for our tomorrow, the after life. What is it that you want out of life? Is it to be free without worries, wars, hate or pain? If it is, what are we doing to make it happen, to make it a reality? Are we working to achieve this feat?

Man has been struggling with this dilemma since he stepped out on his own, and whatever that is to you only you can answer. I like to respond to it this way; ever since man stepped out of the Garden of Eden he has been in a battle for his life. Without God to help us we will always be at each other's throats and our end will be painful. Think about it and let's try to change our direction, one life at a time – but we must believe in the Son, Jesus Christ, in order to make this happen! "Think on these things" are the last four words of Philippians chapter 4, verse 8.

Printed in the United States
122090LV00001B/71/P